First World War Service of John Theodore Morrell

First World War Service of John Theodore Morrell

Christopher D. Cook

Silver Anchor Press · 2025

Published in 2025 by Silver Anchor Press, Berrien Springs, Michigan

ISBN 978-0-9991137-2-1

Contents

Introduction

This book stands as a memorial to John Theodore Morrell, a young farmer from Schuyler County, Illinois, who served his country in Europe during the First World War and returned to start a family and live a long life. He was fortunate; too many were not.

John did not participate in any infamous battles nor was he physically wounded; in fact he never saw combat. This does not mean his experience of war is less important to history than anyone else who served. Every veteran's story is a part of the whole.

John died two months before my third birthday and, unfortunately, I don't remember him. I know of him through family stories and photographs. He and his wife, Millie, were long known as "Grandpa and Grandma Swinger" in our family because they loved to sit on their porch swing in Sciota, Illinois. While he was alive, five generations of the family lived in that small village.

John and Millie left a prodigious family legacy of well over a hundred descendants. It is my hope that this book will help those descendants far into the future to know a bit about their progenitor who left the family farm, went to war, and came back to give us all life.

— C. D. C

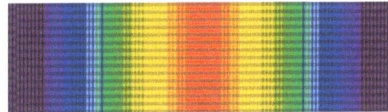

First World War Victory Medal service ribbon.

Portrait of John Theodore Morrell in uniform, sometime after his marriage on 23 Oct 1919 (note wedding band on left hand).

Timeline of Service

1894 Jul 19	John Theodore Morrell is born in Camden Township, Schuyler County, Illinois, the second son of Cyrus Alphonso Morrell and Nora Jane (Marshall) Morrell.[1]
1917 Apr 6	The United States declares war on Germany.
1917 Jun 5	John, a farm laborer working for his uncle, Allie Morrell, is among the more than 1,000 young men of Schuyler County who register for the draft on the first national registration day; he will be placed in Class I (eligible and liable for military service).[2]
1918 May	After almost a year of agricultural deferment, John and his uncle, Grover Cleveland Morrell, are called up in the draft.[3]

"Many of the young men called at this time were actively engaged in farming, but the necessity for recruits is so great that it was necessary to take them to fill the quota."[4]

1918 May 26	Members of the Rebekah and I.O.O.F. lodges hold a supper and entertainment for Schuyler County recruits who will be departing for service the next morning.[5]
1918 May 27	John departs Rushville by rail for Camp Shelby, Hattiesburg, Mississippi, as part of the largest group of draftees (61) sent from Schuyler County at one time.[6]
1918 May 28	John is inducted into the United States Army.[7]
1918 Jun 8	John's grandfather and namesake, Theodore Morrell, dies age 84.[8]

1918 Jun 17	While at Camp Shelby, John is assigned to the 38th Division, 76th Infantry Brigade, 151st Infantry Regiment, Company F, as a private, serial no. 1571430.[9]
1918 Jul 19	John turns twenty-four at Camp Shelby.
1918 Sep 30	John's company completes training at Camp Shelby and travels by rail to Camp Mills, New York, in preparation for deployment to Europe.[10]
1918 Oct 5	John's company moves from Camp Mills to Montreal, Canada.[11]
1918 Oct 12	John's company boards the British ship *Nagoya* in Quebec.[12]
1918 Oct 14	*Nagoya* sails from Quebec bound for England.[13]
1918 Oct 26	*Nagoya* arrives in Gravesend, England.[14]

The British passenger/cargo liner *Nagoya*, launched in 1913, was owned and operated by the Peninsular and Oriental Steam Navigation Company (P&O) for Far East service. Like thousands of other merchant ships, it was requisitioned for wartime use and became a troop transport ship. Nearly half of the American soldiers sent to France traveled on British ships.[15]

Detail from a peacetime postcard of *Nagoya* in port at Yokohama, Japan.

1918 Oct 29	John's company passes through Winnall Down transit camp near Winchester, England, before sailing from Southampton to cross the English Channel.[16]
1918 Oct 30	John's company arrives in Le Havre, France.[17]
1918 Nov 5	With John's company now skeletonized, he is transferred to the 83rd Division, 2nd Depot, Le Mans, France, where troops receive further training and reassignment before being forwarded to the front.[18]

Soldiers in the kitchen and mess line at Le Mans forwarding camp, 3 Mar 1919.

1918 Nov 11	Armistice goes into effect at 11:00 AM ending fighting on the Western Front where nearly two million American soldiers are serving.
1918 Dec 1	Allied troops—including a quarter million Americans—begin to enter Germany commencing the occupation of the Rhineland that will last until 1923.[19]
1919 Feb	John is mustered with the 4th Division, 7th Infantry Brigade, 39th Infantry Regiment, Company D, in Germany.[20]
1919 Apr 4	Company D is at Remagen, Germany.[21]
1919 Apr 10	Company D is at Rolandseck, Germany.[22]
1919 May 23	Company D is at Bitburg, Germany.[23]
1919 Jun 28	Treaty of Versailles ends the war and sets in motion the demobilization of most American troops.

1919 Jul 9	John's division moves to Brest, France.[24]
1919 Jul 19	John turns twenty-five in France.
1919 Jul 30	After nine months in Europe, John sails from Brest on the ship *Leviathan*, bound for the United States.[25]
1919 Aug 6	*Leviathan* arrives at Hoboken, New Jersey.[26]

The German passenger liner *Vaterland*, launched in 1913, was owned and operated by the Hamburg America Line until it was seized at port in Hoboken by the U.S. government on 6 Apr 1917. When launched, *Vaterland* was the largest passenger liner in the world. The U.S. renamed the vessel *Leviathan* and converted it into a transport ship capable of carrying up to 14,000 troops.[27]

Leviathan sporting "dazzle" camouflage at Brest, France, 30 May 1918.

1919 Aug 10	John is transferred to Camp Grant, Rockford, Illinois.[28]
1919 Aug 13	John is honorably discharged from the Army at Camp Grant and receives his final pay totaling $83.45 (equivalent to $1,513 in 2024) which includes a $60 bonus and $9.85 pay to cover his rail ticket home to Rushville. He has no wounds, is in good physical condition, and of very good character.[29]
1919 Sep 18	Residents of Schuyler County organize the first annual "Day of Smiles" celebration in Rushville to honor veterans and to welcome home returning servicemembers.[30]
1919 Oct 23	John marries Melvina Permelia "Millie" Irwin in Rushville.[31]
1985 May 12	John dies at the Veterans Administration Hospital in Iowa City, Iowa, aged ninety, and is buried with military rites beside his late wife at Forest Lawn Cemetery in Macomb, Illinois. He is survived by five of his seven

children, twenty-five grandchildren, forty-eight great-grandchildren, ten great-great-grandchildren, four step-grandchildren, three step-great-grandchildren, and five step-great-great-grandchildren. He was a member of the American Legion Post No. 424 in Blandinville, Illinois.[32]

Portrait of John Theodore Morrell in civilian clothing, possibly early 1918.

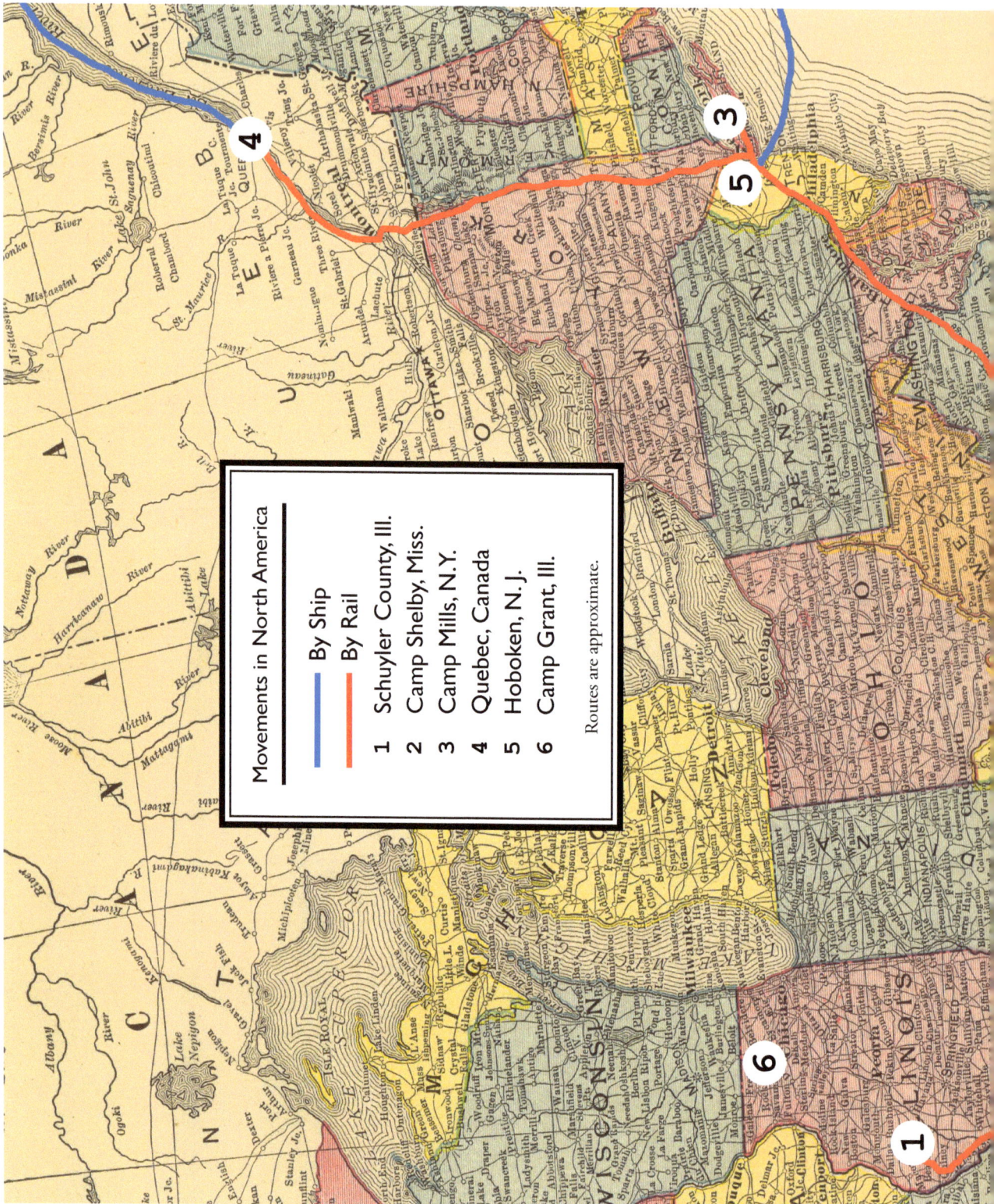

Movements in North America

— By Ship
— By Rail

1 Schuyler County, Ill.
2 Camp Shelby, Miss.
3 Camp Mills, N.Y.
4 Quebec, Canada
5 Hoboken, N.J.
6 Camp Grant, Ill.

Routes are approximate.

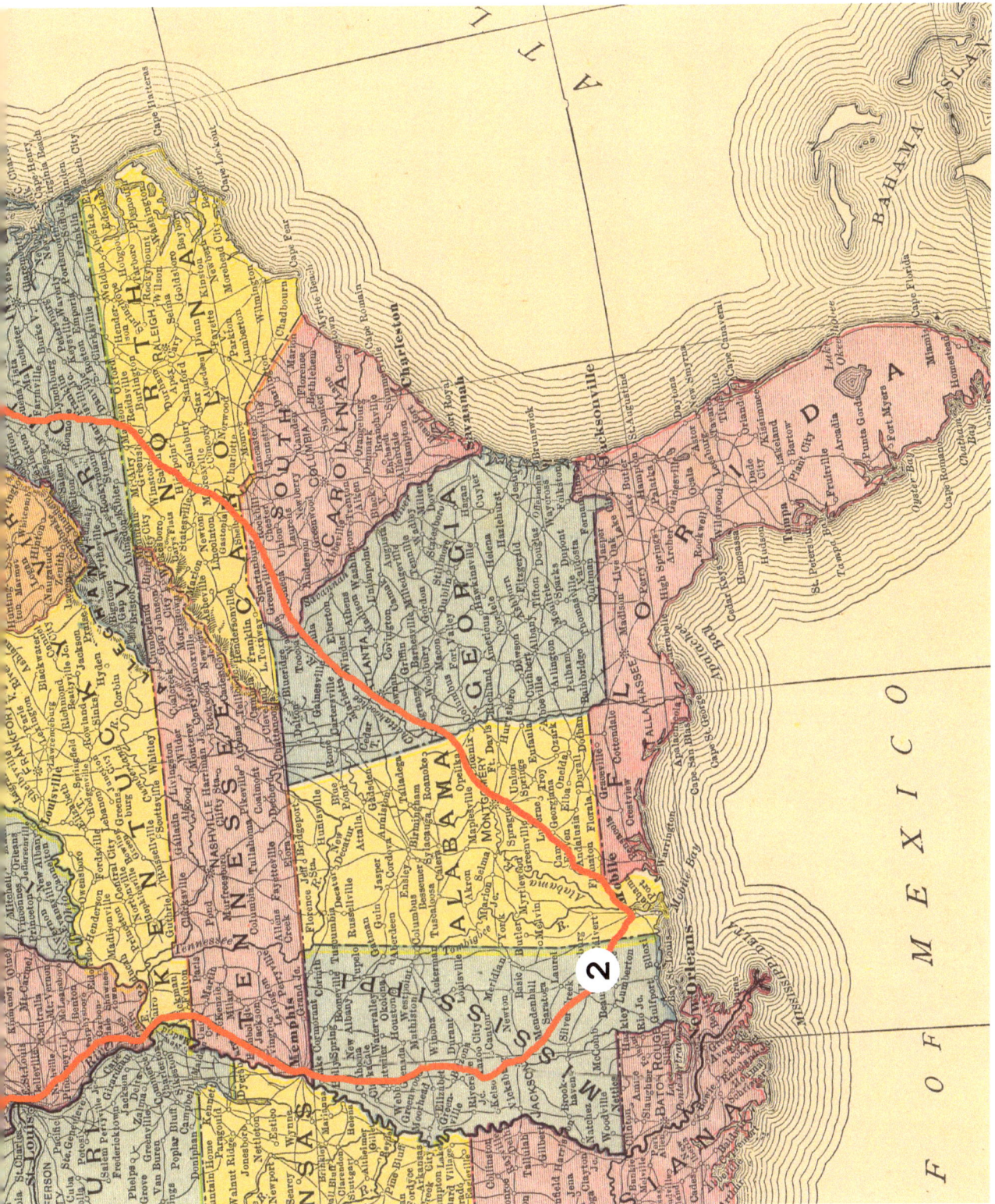

1
2
3
4
5
GREAT BRITAIN
NORTH SEA
ENGLAND
WALES
IRISH SEA
NORTHERN IRELAND
NETHERLANDS
BELGIUM
LUXEMBOURG
ALSACE
SAAR BASIN
CHANNEL IS. (Br.)
HELGOLAND (Ger.)
FRISIAN IS.
Dogger Bank
Strait of Dover
English Channel
Bristol Channel
St. George's Channel
Firth of Forth
London
Dover
Brighton
Portsmouth
Southampton
Plymouth
Bristol
Oxford
Cardiff
Swansea
Birmingham
Leicester
Nottingham
Manchester
Liverpool
Leeds
York
Hull
Newcastle
Sunderland
Edinburgh
Glasgow
Dundee
Perth
Paisley
Belfast
Londonderry
Dublin
Norwich
The Wash
Humber
Calais
Ostend
Bruges
Lille
Brussels
Ghent
Antwerp
Liege
Rotterdam
The Hague
Amsterdam
Groningen
Zuider Zee
Le Havre
Rouen
Amiens
Cherbourg
Paris
Versailles
Reims
Le Mans
Orleans
Rennes
Nantes
Angers
Brest
Metz
Nancy
Strasbourg
Mulhouse
Cologne
Coblenz
Wiesbaden
Mainz
Frankfurt
Darmstadt
Mannheim
Karlsruhe
Dusseldorf
Duisburg
Essen
Dortmund
Elberfeld
Munster
Osnabruck
Hanover
Bremen
Wilhelmshaven
Altona
Lubeck
Kiel
SLESVIG
Horsens
Aarhus
Odense
FYEN
DENMARK
Seine R.
Loire R.
Marne R.
Oise R.
Meuse R.
Rhine R.
Weser R.
Ems R.
Elbe
USHANT
BELLE ILE
London–Oslo
London–Copenhagen
Hamburg–Copenhagen
Hamburg–Buenos Aires
London–Bordeaux
Plymouth–Bordeaux

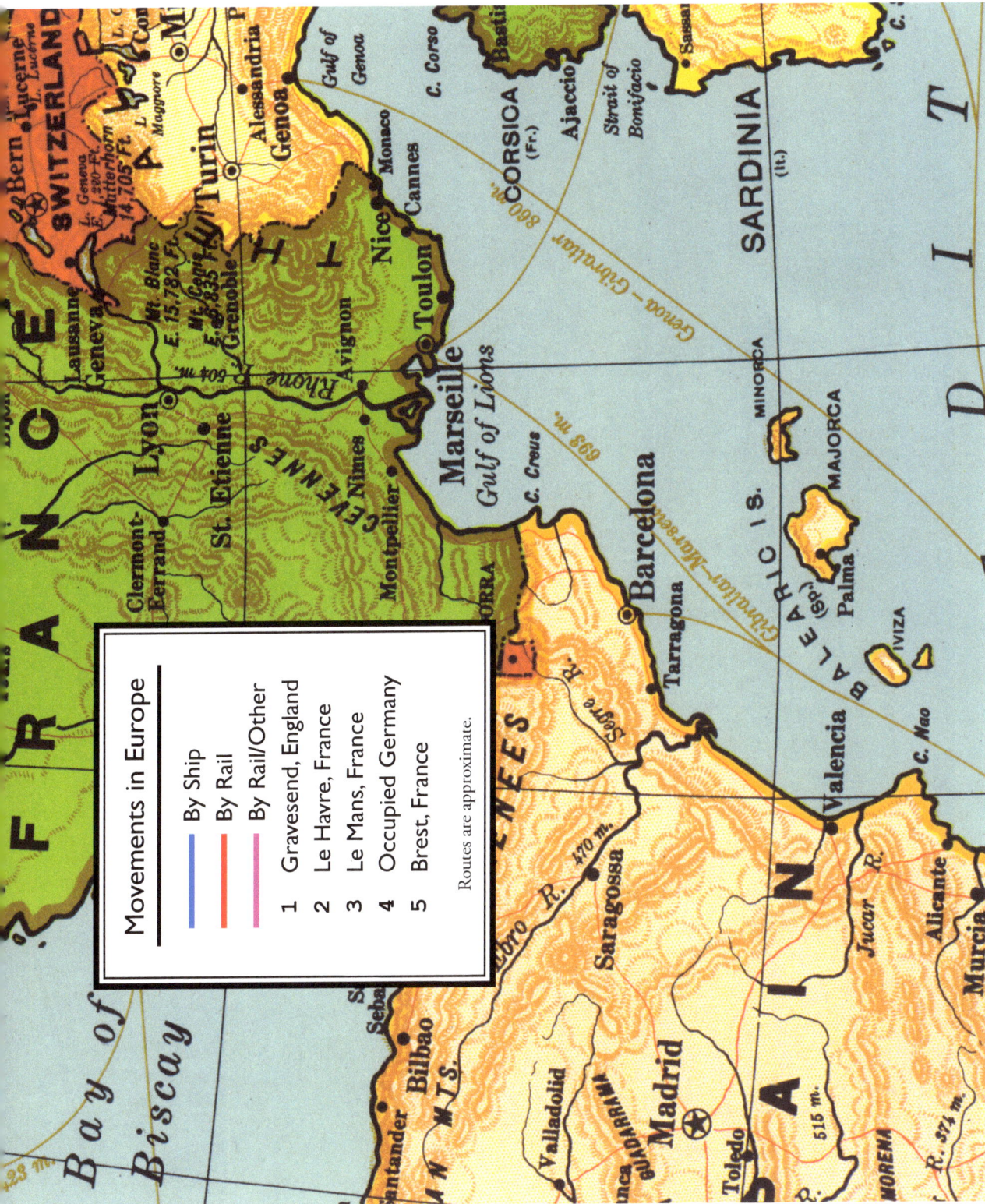

Movements in Europe

— By Ship
— By Rail
— By Rail/Other

1 Gravesend, England
2 Le Havre, France
3 Le Mans, France
4 Occupied Germany
5 Brest, France

Routes are approximate.

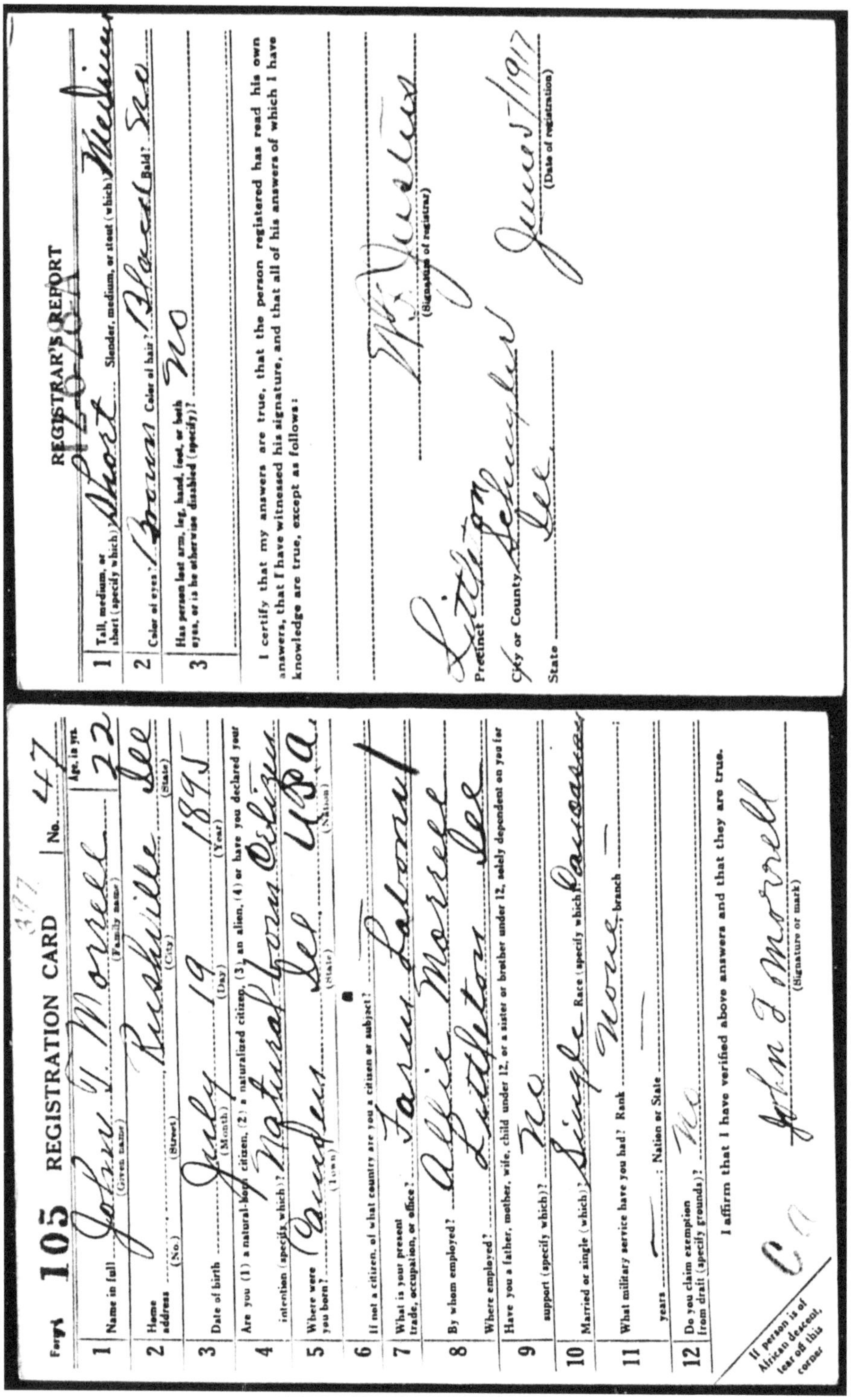

Form 1 105 REGISTRATION CARD No. 47

1 Name in full John T. Morrell (Given name) (Family name) Age, in yrs. 22

2 Home address (No.) (Street) Rushville Ill (City) (State)

3 Date of birth July 19 1895 (Month) (Day) (Year)

4 Are you (1) a natural-born citizen, (2) a naturalized citizen, (3) an alien, (4) or have you declared your intention (specify which)? Natural born Citizen

5 Where were you born? Camden Ill U.S.A. (Town) (State) (Nation)

6 If not a citizen, of what country are you a citizen or subject?

7 What is your present trade, occupation, or office? Farm Laborer

8 By whom employed? Allie Morrell
Where employed? Littleton Ill

9 Have you a father, mother, wife, child under 12, or a sister or brother under 12, solely dependent on you for support (specify which)? No

10 Married or single (which)? Single Race (specify which)? Caucasian

11 What military service have you had? Rank None; branch —
years —; Nation or State

12 Do you claim exemption from draft (specify grounds)? No

I affirm that I have verified above answers and that they are true.

John T Morrell (Signature or mark)

If person is of African descent, tear off this corner

REGISTRAR'S REPORT

1 Tall, medium, or short (specify which)? Short Slender, medium, or stout (which)? Medium

2 Color of eyes? Brown Color of hair? Black Bald? No

3 Has person lost arm, leg, hand, foot, or both eyes, or is he otherwise disabled (specify)? No

I certify that my answers are true, that the person registered has read his own answers, that I have witnessed his signature, and that all of his answers of which I have knowledge are true, except as follows:

W. Justus (Signature of registrar)

Precinct Littleton
City or County Schuyler
State Ill

June 5/1917 (Date of registration)

John Theodore Morrell's draft registration card, 5 Jun 1917.

CERTIFIED COPY OF HONORABLE DISCHARGE

RECORD OF
HONORABLE DISCHARGE
FROM
The United States Army

TO ALL WHOM IT MAY CONCERN:

This Is To Certify, that......John T. Morrell.............
1571430 Private Company "D" 39th Infantry....
......................, as a TESTIMONIAL OF HONEST AND FAITH-
FUL SERVICE, is hereby HONORABLY DISCHARGED from the military service of the UNITED
STATES by reason of....Convenience of the Government, Demobilization of
Organization, Per Circular 106, W.D. 1918......
Said......John T. Morrell.....
was born in......Camden......, in the State of......Illinois....
When enlisted he was 23 10/12 years of age, and by occupation a......Farmer....
He had....Brown........eyes,.....Black........hair,.......Dark.......complexion, and was
.....5.......feet......6.....inches in height.
Given under my hand at......Camp Grant, Illinois........this.....13th.....day
of....August......, one thousand nine hundred and......Nineteen.......

Wm. Smith
Major Inf. U.S.A.
Commanding.

ENLISTMENT RECORD

Name:....John T. Morrell..........................Grade:....Private....
Enlisted or inducted 5-28-1918 at......Rushville, Illinois......
Serving in.......First.........................enlistment period at date of discharge.
Prior Service: .....None.....

Noncommissioned officer : .....None.....

:Transportation Issued:
C. B. & Q. R. R.
Aug. 13, 1919
Camp Grant

Marksmanship, gunner qualification or rating :.....None.....   :   1   Ill   1 :
Horsemanship : .....None.....
Battles, engagements, skirmishes, expeditions :.....None   A E F.....
Decoration; Badges;.....None.....
Medals; Citations;.....None.....
Knowledge of any vocation :.....Farmer.....
Wounds received in service :.....None.....
Physical condition when discharged :.....Good.....
Typhoid prophylaxis completed.....5-31-18.....
Paratyphoid prophylaxis completed.....5-31-18.....
Married or single :.....Single.....
CHARACTER:.....Very Good.....
Remarks: .....Entitled to travel pay to Rushville, Ill.....
Sailed from U. S. 10-12-18; Returned to U.S. 8-6-19. Absence without
leave under G.O. No. 31, W.D. 1912 and No. 45, W.D. 1914; None
Signature of Soldier:.....John T. Morrell.....
Camp Grant, Ill, Aug. 13-1919
Paid in full $83.45
Including Bonus of $60.00 Act of February 24-1919
P. G. Hoyt-Major Q.M.C.
Per M. Peterson
2nd Lieut. Q.M.C. Paid T.P. to Rushville, Ill.

HARRISON M. HUTCHINGS
Captain Inf.
Commanding......Demob. Group

Filed for Record the 13th day of January, A.D., 1923, at 2 o'clock P. M.
No. 98836   L. H. Byrns, Recorder.

John Theodore Morrell's certified copy of honorable discharge.

The United States of America

honors the memory of

JOHN T. MORRELL

This certificate is awarded by a grateful nation in recognition of devoted and selfless consecration to the service of our country in the Armed Forces of the United States.

Ronald Reagan
President of the United States

John Theodore Morrell's presidential memorial certificate.

Obituary

John T. Morrell

SCIOTA - Graveside funeral services will be held at 9:30 a.m. Thursday at Forest Lawn Memory Gardens, Macomb, for John T. Morrell, 90, of Sciota who died at 1:25 p.m. Sunday in the Veterans Administration Hospital in Iowa City.

Virgil Kelly will officiate at the services and military rites will be conducted there.

Friends may call after 8 a.m. Tuesday at the Sergeant-Worthington Funeral Home in Macomb, where the family will visit with friends from 7 to 9 p.m. Tuesday.

He was born July 19, 1894 in Schuyler County, the son of Cyrus and Nora Marshall Morrell. He married Millie Irwin in Rushville on Oct. 23, 1919. She died Jan. 8, 1979.

He is survived by a son, Gene Morrell of Sciota; four daughters, Mrs. Robert (Carol) Cobb of Macomb, Mrs. Juanita Senn and Mrs. Ralph (Alice) Smith, both of Burlington, Iowa and Mrs. Harry (Eva) Drummond of Good Hope.

He is also survived by 25 grandchildren, 48 great-grandchildren, 10 great-great-grandchildren, four step-grandchildren, three step-great-grandchildren and five step-great-great-grandchildren.

A daughter, Ruth; a son, Jimmie; five brothers, Perry, William, Homer, Charles and Richard and three sisters, Mrs. Alta Seth, Mrs. Mary Atkisson [i.e., Adkison] and Sadie Reeder died earlier.

An Army veteran of World War I, he was a member of the Blandinsville American Legion Post No. 424.

He had been a farmer and also worked at the Macomb Steel Co. and the Hemp Co. in Macomb as well as Mickleberry's [i.e., Mickelberry Food Products Co.] and the Norcross Co. in Bushnell.

Memorials may be made to the charity of the donor's choice.[33]

Portrait of John Theodore
Morrell and Melvina Permelia
"Millie" (Irwin) Morrell.

Children of John Theodore Morrell and Melvina Permelia "Millie" (Irwin) Morrell

Juanita Mae Morrell was born on 17 Oct 1920 in Schuyler County, Illinois, and died on 12 Mar 1996 in Rockford, Winnebago County, Illinois, aged seventy-five years.[34]

Ruth Aileen Morrell was born on 21 Oct 1922 in Schuyler County, Illinois, and died there on 4 Feb 1923, aged three months and fourteen days.[35]

Clyde Eugene "Gene" Morrell was born on 21 Jan 1924 in Littleton, Schuyler County, Illinois, and died on 19 Jul 1990 in Springfield, Sangamon County, Illinois, aged sixty-six years.[36]

Jimmie Eldon Morrell was born on 15 Sep 1929 in Illinois and died on 1 Dec 1962 in Garland, Dallas County, Texas, aged thirty-three years.[37]

Alice Maxine Morrell was born on 3 Nov 1931 in McDonough County, Illinois, and died on 20 Dec 1999 in Macomb, McDonough County, Illinois, aged sixty-eight years.[38]

Carol Lee Morrell was born on 7 Nov 1934 in Grand Junction, Mesa County, Colorado, and died on 17 Oct 2023 in Springfield, Sangamon County, Illinois, aged eighty-eight years.[39]

Eva Jayne Morrell was born on 19 Aug 1936 in Sciota, McDonough County, Illinois, and died on 17 Oct 2018 in Macomb, McDonough County, Illinois, aged eighty-two years.[40]

Portrait of John Theodore Morrell with his granddaughter, Jeanette Marie Morrell, 1947.

Portrait of five generations gathered for Christmas in 1982, from left to right: Christopher Duane Cook, Tammy Suzanne (Rigg) Cook, Clyde Eugene Morrell, Jeanette Marie (Morrell) Rigg, and John Theodore Morrell.

John Theodore Morrell's grave marker at Forest Lawn Cemetery (plot Good Shepherd 104-A-3), Macomb, Illinois.

Endnotes

1. *Illinois, World War I Selective Service System Draft Registration Cards, 1917–1918*, Schuyler County, John T. Morrell (FamilySearch Library [hereinafter FSL] DGS 5248817, image 1881 of 4792) (place of birth: "Camden, Ill."; has year of birth as "1895" in error); *Illinois, Selective Service System Registration Cards [World War II]: Fourth Registration*, John Theodore Morrell (FSL DGS 4134827, images 5197–5198 of 6142) (middle name: "Theodore"); "John T. Morrell [obituary]," *Macomb Daily Journal* (Macomb, Ill.), 13 May 1985, sec. 1, p. 3; 1900 U.S. Census, Camden Twp., Schuyler Co., Ill., sheet B11, family 238, household of Cyrus L. [*sic*] Morrell.

2. *Illinois, World War I Selective Service System Draft Registration Cards, 1917–1918*, Schuyler County, John T. Morrell (FSL DGS 5248817, image 1881 of 4792) (has year of birth as "1895" in error); "No Slackers in Evidence: More Than One Thousand Young Men Register in Schuyler," *Rushville Times* (Rushville, Ill.), 7 Jun 1917, p. [1]; "Last Questionnaires Mailed: Schuyler County Registrants Will Be Classified in Ten Days," *Rushville Times* (Rushville, Ill.), 10 Jan 1918, p. [1].

3. "Summon 116 Selectives: Schuyler County Called Upon for Three Drafts for the Army," *Rushville Times* (Rushville, Ill.), 23 May 1918, p. [1], 4; "Leave for Southern Camps: Schuyler sends 116 Recruits into Camp within Seven Days, *Rushville Times* (Rushville, Ill.), 30 May 1918, p. [1].

4. "Summon 116 Selectives: Schuyler County Called Upon for Three Drafts for the Army," *Rushville Times* (Rushville, Ill.), 23 May 1918, p. [1].

5. "Leave for Southern Camps: Schuyler sends 116 Recruits into Camp within Seven Days, *Rushville Times* (Rushville, Ill.), 30 May 1918, p. [1].

6. Ibid.

7. Schuyler Co., Ill., Certified Copy of Honorable Discharge of John T. Morrell, filed 13 Jan 1923, certificate no. 98836, reissued 16 May 1950.

8. Schuyler Co., Ill., Death Certificate of Theodore Morrell, filed 30 Jun 1918; "Death of an Old Resident [obituary of Theodore Morrell]," *Rushville Times* (Rushville, Ill.), 13 Jun 1918, p. 5.

9. *United States, World War I, Military Muster Rolls and Rosters, 1916–1939*, World War I Rosters of Enlisted Men, 150th–152nd Inf Regt, Reel 14.245, Roll 394, 1916–1939, "Muster Roll of Company F of the 151st Infantry at Camp Shelby, Miss., from the last bimonthly muster on April 30, 1918, to the muster on June 30, 1918" (FSL DGS 106285402, images 986–1001 of 2011); *Order of Battle of the United States Land Forces in the World War*, vol. 2, *American Expeditionary Forces: Divisions* (Washington, D.C.: Center of Military History, United States Army, 1988), p. 241.

10. *United States, World War I, Military Muster Rolls and Rosters, 1916–1939*, World War I Rosters of Enlisted Men, 150th–152nd Inf Regt, Reel 14.245, Roll 394, 1916–1939, "Roster of Company (F) 151st Infantry at Midnight September [30, 1918]" (FSL DGS 106285402, images 1010–1013 of 2011); *Order of Battle of the United States Land Forces in the World War*, vol. 3, pt. 3, *Zone of the Interior: Directory of Troops* (Washington, D.C.: Center of Military History, United States Army, 1988), p. 367; Eric B. Setzekorn, *Joining the Great War, April 1917–April 1918* (Washington, D.C.: Center of Military History, United States Army, 2017), p. 30 ("On completion of their training, soldiers boarded troop trains for the journey to the East Coast where they would await transport across the Atlantic.").

11. Inferred from muster roll dates of hospital transfers at Camp Mills (1–4 Oct) and Montreal (5–11 Oct): *United States, World War I, Military Muster Rolls and Rosters, 1916–1939*, World War I Rosters of Enlisted Men, 150th–152nd Inf Regt, Reel 14.245, Roll 394, 1916–1939, "Company F, 151st Infantry, Coulans, France, November 14, 1918" (FSL DGS 106285402, images 1015–1020 of 2011).

12. *U.S., Army Transport Service Arriving and Departing Passenger Lists, 1910–1939*, Outgoing, Nagoya, 9 Sep 1918–1919 (Ancestry.com, collection 61174, images 106, 113, and 158 of 224).

13. *U.S., Army Transport Service Arriving and Departing Passenger Lists, 1910–1939*, Outgoing, Nagoya, 9 Sep 1918–1919 (Ancestry.com, collection 61174, images 106, 113, and 158 of 224); Registry of Shipping and Seamen: Ships' Official Logs, Extracted Logs: Ship's Name *Nagoya*, Official Number 135323, Dates of Voyages [. . .] 24 August 1918–27 October 1918, The National Archives, Kew, England, BT 165/1860.

14. Registry of Shipping and Seamen: Ships' Official Logs, Extracted Logs: Ship's Name *Nagoya*, Official Number 135323, Dates of Voyages [. . .] 24 August 1918–27 October 1918, The National Archives, Kew, England, BT 165/1860.

15. "NAGOYA (1913)," P&O Heritage, https://poheritage.com/collections/3a08f780-7916-31f8-8f1c-3a09dee976f9; Paul B. Cora and Alexander A. Falbo-Wild, *Supporting Allied Offensives, 8 August–11 November 1918* (Washington, D.C.: Center of Military History, United States Army, 2018), p. 8.

16. Inferred from muster roll dates of hospital transfers at Winnall Down (29 Oct) and Le Havre (30 Oct–2 Nov): *United States, World War I, Military Muster Rolls and Rosters, 1916–1939*, World War I Rosters of Enlisted Men, 150th–152nd Inf Regt, Reel 14.245, Roll 394, 1916–1939, "Company F, 151st Infantry, Coulans, France, November 14, 1918" (FSL DGS 106285402, images 1015–1020 of 2011); Erin Standing, "Winchester During Modern War," *Culture on Call*, Hampshire Cultural Trust, 7 Jun 2024, https://www.cultureoncall.com/winchester-wars.

17. Inferred from muster roll dates of hospital transfers at Winnall Down (29 Oct) and Le Havre (30 Oct–2 Nov): *United States, World War I, Military Muster Rolls and Rosters, 1916–1939*, World War I Rosters of Enlisted Men, 150th–152nd Inf Regt, Reel 14.245, Roll 394, 1916–1939, "Company F, 151st Infantry, Coulans, France, November 14, 1918" (FSL DGS 106285402, images 1015–1020 of 2011).

18. *United States, World War I, Military Muster Rolls and Rosters, 1916–1939*, World War I Rosters of Enlisted Men, 150th–152nd Inf Regt, Reel 14.245, Roll 394, 1916–1939, "Company F, 151st Infantry, Cou-

lans, France, November 14, 1918" (FSL DGS 106285402, images 1015–1020 of 2011); *Order of Battle of the United States Land Forces in the World War*, vol. 2, *American Expeditionary Forces: Divisions* (Washington, D.C.: Center of Military History, United States Army, 1988), p. 245; *Order of Battle of the United States Land Forces in the World War*, vol. 3, pt. 3, *Zone of the Interior: Directory of Troops* (Washington, D.C.: Center of Military History, United States Army, 1988), p. 1391.

19. *The Medical Department of the United States Army in the World War*, vol. 8, Charles Lynch, Joseph H. Ford, and Frank W. Weed, *Field Operations* (Washington, D.C.: Government Printing Office, 1925), p. 897; Brian F. Neumann and Shane D. Makowicki, *Occupation and Demobilization, 1918–1923* (Washington, D.C.: Center of Military History, United States Army, 2019), p. 7, 17.

20. *United States, World War I, Military Muster Rolls and Rosters, 1916–1939*, World War I Rosters of Enlisted Men, 39th Inf Regt, Reel 18.114, Roll 281, 1916–1939, "Roster of Company 'D' 39th Infantry: Correct as of midnight Febuary [sic] 28th, 1919" (FSL DGS 106281612, images 1291–1294 of 1930); *Order of Battle of the United States Land Forces in the World War*, vol. 2, *American Expeditionary Forces: Divisions* (Washington, D.C.: Center of Military History, United States Army, 1988), p. 60.

An exhaustive search of muster rolls did not locate John Morrell in December 1918 or January 1919. The rolls for the 39th Inf., Co. D., for December and January were signed at Kempenich, Germany (FSL DGS 106281612, images 1286 and 1289 of 1930). Rolls for February 1919 onward—on which John Morrell does appear—do not give a location but are signed by the same personnel adjutant, Clarence J. Wittbecker, as in January.

21. Robert B. Cole and Barnard Eberlin, eds., *The History of the 39th U.S. Infantry During the World War* (New York: Press of Joseph D. McGuire, 1919), p. 137.

22. Ibid.

23. Ibid.

24. *Order of Battle of the United States Land Forces in the World War*, vol. 2, *American Expeditionary Forces: Divisions* (Washington, D.C.: Center of Military History, United States Army, 1988), p. 73.

25. *U.S., Army Transport Service Arriving and Departing Passenger Lists, 1910–1939*, Incoming, Leviathan, 25 Jul 1919–6 Aug 1919 (Ancestry. com, collection 61174, images 586 and 670 *inter alia* of 875).

26. Ibid.

27. "SS *Vaterland* (1913)," Wikipedia, last modified 3 Apr 2025, 02:42 (UTC), https://en.wikipedia.org/wiki/SS_Vaterland_(1913).

28. *United States, World War I, Military Muster Rolls and Rosters, 1916–1939*, World War I Rosters of Enlisted Men, 39th Inf Regt, Reel 18.114, Roll 281, 1916–1939, "Roster of Company 'D' Thirty Ninth Infantry: Correct as of midnight August 31st, 1919" (FSL DGS 106281612, images 1315–1319 of 1930).

29. Schuyler Co., Ill., Certified Copy of Honorable Discharge of John T. Morrell, filed 13 Jan 1923, certificate no. 98836, reissued 16 May 1950; Final Payment Roll, Demobilization Group, Camp Grant, Illinois, 13 Aug 1919, National Personnel Records Center, St. Louis, Mo.

30. "Hail! Hail! The Gang's All Here!," *Rushville Times* (Rushville, Ill.), 18 Sep 1919, p. [1]; "They Smiled Amid the Rain: Rushville's Welcome to Her Soldier Boys Was Welcome Tho Wet," *Rushville Times* (Rushville, Ill.), 25 Sep 1919, p. [1].

31. Schuyler Co., Ill., Marriage Certificate of John T. Morrell and Melvina Irwin, filed 23 Oct 1919.

32. Johnson Co., Iowa, Death Certificate of John Theodore Morrell, filed 15 May 1985 (has state of birth as "Iowa" in error); "John T. Morrell [obituary]," *Macomb Daily Journal* (Macomb, Ill.), 13 May 1985, sec. 1, p. 3.

33. "John T. Morrell [obituary]," *Macomb Daily Journal* (Macomb, Ill.), 13 May 1985, sec. 1, p. 3.

34. "Juanita Senn [obituary]," *Henderson County Quill* (Stronghurst, Ill.), 20 Mar 1996, p. 10.

35. Schuyler Co., Ill., Death Certificate of Ruth Aileen Morrell, filed 6 Feb 1923.

36. Illinois, Department of Public Health, Delayed Record of Birth, state file no. 200376 (born 1924, filed 1962), Clyde Eugene Morrell; "Clyde Morrell [obituary]," *Macomb Journal* (Macomb, Ill.), 20 Jul 1990, p. 2.

37. Dallas County, Texas, Death Certificate of Jimmie Eldon Morrell, filed 5 Dec 1962; "Cyclist Second Traffic Victim," *Daily-News and Times Reporter* (Garland, Texas), 3 Dec 1962, p. 1, 8.

38. "Alice Smith [obituary]," *Peoria Journal Star* (Peoria, Ill.), 21 Dec 1999, p. B05; middle name from interview with Jeanette Marie (Morrell) Ingersoll, 24 May 2025.

39. "Official Obituary of Carol L. Cobb," Clugston-Tibbitts Funeral Home, 23 Oct 2023, https://www.clugston-tibbitts.com/obituary/Carol-Cobb; middle name from interview with Jeanette Marie (Morrell) Ingersoll, 24 May 2025.

40. United States, Obituary Records, 2014–2023, "Obituary for Eva Jayne Drummond," 18 Oct 2018, https://www.familysearch.org/ark:/61903/1:1:61XB-JC27.

Illustration Credits

Page 7: "First World War Victory Medal service ribbon." *File:World War I Victory Medal ribbon.svg*. Wikimedia Commons. https://commons. wikimedia.org/w/index.php?title=File:World_War_I_Victory_Medal_ ribbon.svg&oldid=915194238.

Page 8: "Portrait of John Theodore Morrell in uniform, sometime after his marriage on 23 Oct 1919 (note wedding band on left hand)." Photographer unknown; undated. Original in the collection of Christopher D. Cook.

Page 10: "Detail from a peacetime postcard of *Nagoya* in port at Yokohama, Japan." Artist and publisher unknown; undated. Original in the collection of Christopher D. Cook.

Page 11: "Soldiers in the kitchen and mess line at Le Mans forwarding camp, 3 Mar 1919." Jones, T. F. *30th Division [. . .] Forwarding Camp, Le Mans, Sarthe, France*. Photographs of American Military Archives, Records of the Office of the Chief Signal Officer, National Archives and Records Administration, identifier 313155882. https://catalog.archives. gov/id/313155882.

Page 12: "*Leviathan* sporting 'dazzle' camouflage at Brest, France, 30 May 1918." *File:USS Leviathan being used to transport American troops, Brest, France, May 30, 1918 (28294620966).jpg*. Wikimedia Commons. https://commons.wikimedia.org/w/index.php?title=File:USS_ Leviathan_being_used_to_transport_American_troops,_Brest,_ France,_May_30,_1918_(28294620966).jpg&oldid=955832777.

Page 13: "Portrait of John Theodore Morrell in civilian clothing, possibly early 1918." Photographer unknown; undated. Original in the collection of Christopher D. Cook.

Pages 14–15: Map: "Movements in North America." Detail, altered, from: *Rand-McNally's New 14 × 21 Map of the United States.* [Chicago]: Rand-McNally & Co., 1912. David Rumsey Map Collection, David Rumsey Map Center, Stanford Libraries, list no. 3490.003. https://www.davidrumsey.com/luna/servlet/s/3q1c0b.

Pages 16–17: Map: "Movements in Europe." Detail, altered, from: Bacon, G. W. *Bacon's Standard Map of Europe.* [Chicago Heights, Ill.]: Weber Costello Co., [1925?]. World Digital Library, Library of Congress. http://hdl.loc.gov/loc.gmd/g5700.ct001973.

Page 18: "John Theodore Morrell's draft registration card, 5 Jun 1917." *Illinois, World War I Selective Service System Draft Registration Cards, 1917–1918,* Schuyler County, John T. Morrell (FSL DGS 5248817, image 1881 of 4792).

Page 19: "John Theodore Morrell's certified copy of honorable discharge." Original in the collection of Christopher D. Cook.

Page 20: "John Theodore Morrell's presidential memorial certificate." Original in the collection of Christopher D. Cook.

Page 22: "Portrait of John Theodore Morrell and Melvina Permelia 'Millie' (Irwin) Morrell." Photographer unknown; undated. Original in the collection of Christopher D. Cook.

Page 24: "Portrait of John Theodore Morrell with his granddaughter, Jeanette Marie Morrell, 1947." Photographer unknown; dated 1947 on verso. Original in the collection of Christopher D. Cook.

Page 24: "Portrait of five generations . . . ." Photographer unknown; dated 1982 on verso. Original in the collection of Christopher D. Cook.

Page 25: "John Theodore Morrell's grave marker . . . ." Photograph by Christopher D. Cook; taken 4 Jul 2024. Digital original in the collection of Christopher D. Cook.

Index

Page numbers in *italics* refer to illustrations.

www.ingramcontent.com/pod-product-compliance
Lightning Source LLC
Chambersburg PA
CBHW041549260326
41914CB00016B/1590